C000153071

Vegetarian Soup Cool
Plant-Based Soups and ~~Broths for~~
Health and Natural Weight Loss

by **Alissa Noel Grey**
Text copyright(c)2019 Alissa Noel Grey

All rights reserved. No part of this publication may be reproduced, distributed, or transmitted in any form or by any means, including photocopying, recording, or other electronic or mechanical methods, without the prior written permission of the publisher, except in the case of brief quotations embodied in critical reviews and certain other noncommercial uses permitted by copyright law

Although every precaution has been taken to verify the accuracy of the information contained herein, the author and publisher assume no responsibility for any errors or omissions. No liability is assumed for damages that may result from the use of information contained within.

Table Of Contents

Delicious Vegetarian Soups the Whole Family Will Love!

As a working mom of three teenagers and as someone who tries to cook healthy food, while at the same time trying to save time, I am constantly looking for new, different and varied vegetarian soups that can be served for dinner, lunch and even breakfast. My new vegetarian soup cookbook is a collection of some of the best meat-free, protein-packed, soup recipes, that can be prepared on a daily basis. Many of them have been in my family for generations, others are the result of my inspiration and experimentation in order to appeal to contemporary tastes. Good nutrition is the best gift we can give ourselves and our loved ones and my vegetarian soups will provide enough protein, vitamins, minerals and antioxidants to keep you and your family strong and feeling better all-round.

My vegetarian soup recipes include lots of brightly colored vegetables such as eggplants, peppers, tomatoes, avocados and cabbage, superfood legumes, quinoa, and buckwheat as these are some of the healthiest foods on the planet which are, at the same time, wonderfully versatile and easily combined in meals. They are quick to make before or after work, even by inexperienced cooks and once you try them out, you will soon be inspired and start discovering new delicious dishes on your own.

Preparing healthy vegetarian soups for my family is fun as well as rewarding because it is just another way of offering my children a future of well-being and optimum health.

Alkalizing Green Soup

Serves: 4-5
Prep time: 20 min

Ingredients:

2 cups broccoli, cut into florets and chopped

2 zucchinis, peeled and chopped

2 cups chopped kale

1 small onion, chopped

2-3 garlic cloves, chopped

4 cups vegetable broth

2 tbsp extra virgin olive oil

1/2 tsp ground ginger

1/2 tsp ground coriander

1 lime, juiced, to serve

Directions:

Gently heat olive oil in a large saucepan over medium-high heat. Cook onion and garlic for 3-4 minutes until tender. Add ginger and coriander and stir to coat well.

Add in broccoli, zucchinis, kale and vegetable broth. Bring to the boil, then reduce heat and simmer for 15 minutes, stirring from time to time.

Set aside to cool and blend until smooth. Return to pan and cook until heated through. Serve with lime juice.

Superfood Kale Soup

Serves: 4-5
Prep time: 20 min

Ingredients:

1 onion, chopped

2 carrots, chopped

2 cups chopped kale

2-3 garlic cloves, minced

4 cups vegetable broth

2 tbsp extra virgin olive oil

1/2 tsp ground ginger

1 tsp paprika

yogurt, to serve

Directions:

Gently heat olive oil in a large saucepan over medium-high heat. Cook onion, garlic and carrot for 3-4 minutes until tender. Add ginger and paprika and stir to coat well.

Add in kale and vegetable broth. Bring to the boil, then reduce heat and simmer for 15 minutes, stirring from time to time.

Set aside to cool and blend until smooth. Return to pan and cook until heated through. Serve with yogurt.

Spicy Red Pepper and Potato Soup

Serves 4
Prep time: 30 min

Ingredients:

1 onion, chopped

2 garlic cloves, minced

2 carrots, chopped

2 red bell peppers, chopped

2 cups, diced potatoes

4 cups vegetable broth

3 tbsp extra virgin olive oil

1/2 tsp smoked paprika

1/4 tsp ginger

1/2 tsp dried sage

1/2 tsp cinnamon

1/2 tsp nutmeg

salt, to taste

black pepper, to taste

Directions:

Gently heat olive oil in a large saucepan over medium-high heat. Cook onion, garlic, carrot and the peppers together with all the spices for 3-4 minutes, stirring.

Add in potatoes and the broth. Season with salt and black pepper to taste. Cover and simmer for 20 minutes or until the potatoes and carrots are tender.

Mushroom and Kale Soup

Serves: 4-5
Prep time: 30 min

Ingredients:

1 onion, chopped

1 carrot, chopped

1 zucchini, peeled and diced

1 potato, peeled and diced

10 white mushrooms, chopped

1 bunch kale (10 oz), stemmed and coarsely chopped

3 cups vegetable broth

4 tbsp extra virgin olive oil

salt and black pepper. to taste

Directions:

Gently heat olive oil in a large soup pot. Add in onions, carrot and mushrooms and cook until vegetables are tender.

Stir in zucchini, kale and vegetable broth. Season to taste with salt and pepper and simmer for 20 minutes.

Creamy Broccoli and Potato Soup

Serves: 4-5
Prep time: 30 min

Ingredients:

3 cups broccoli, cut into florets and chopped

2 potatoes, peeled and chopped

1 large onion, chopped

3 garlic cloves, minced

1 cup raw cashews

1 cup vegetable broth

4 cups water

3 tbsp extra virgin olive oil

1/2 tsp ground nutmeg

Directions:

Soak cashews in a bowl covered with water for at least 4 hours. Drain water and blend cashews with 1 cup of vegetable broth until smooth. Set aside.

Gently heat olive oil in a large saucepan over medium-high heat. Cook onion and garlic and for 3-4 minutes until tender. Add in broccoli, potato, nutmeg and water. Cover and bring to the boil, then reduce heat and simmer for 20 minutes, stirring from time to time.

Remove from heat and stir in cashew mixture. Blend until smooth, return to pan and cook until heated through.

Creamy Brussels Sprout Soup

Serves: 4-5
Prep time: 30 min

Ingredients:

1 lb frozen Brussels sprouts, thawed

2 potatoes, peeled and chopped

1 large onion, chopped

3 garlic cloves, minced

1 cup raw cashews

4 cups vegetable broth

3 tbsp extra virgin olive oil

1/2 tsp curry powder

salt and black pepper, to taste

Directions:

Soak cashews in a bowl covered with water for at least 4 hours. Drain water and blend cashews with 1 cup of vegetable broth until smooth. Set aside.

Gently heat olive oil in a large saucepan over medium-high heat. Cook onion and garlic and for 3-4 minutes until tender. Add in Brussels sprouts, potato, curry and vegetable broth.

Cover and bring to a boil, then reduce heat and simmer for 20 minutes, stirring from time to time. Remove from heat and stir in cashew mixture.

Blend until smooth, return to pan and cook until heated through.

Creamy Potato Soup

Serves: 4-5
Prep time: 35 min

Ingredients:

6 medium potatoes, cut into small cubes

1 leek, white part only, chopped

1 carrot, chopped

1 zucchini, peeled and chopped

1 celery stalk, chopped

3 cups water

1 cup coconut milk

3 tbsp extra virgin olive oil

salt and black pepper, to taste

Directions:

Gently heat olive oil in a deep saucepan and sauté the onion for 2-3 minutes. Add in potatoes, carrot, zucchini and celery and cook for 2-3 minutes, stirring.

Add in water and salt and bring to a boil, then lower heat and simmer until the vegetables are tender.

Blend until smooth, add coconut milk, blend some more and serve.

Leek, Brown Rice and Potato Soup

Serves: 4-5
Prep time: 35 min

Ingredients:

3 potatoes, peeled and diced

2 leeks, finely chopped

1/4 cup brown rice

5 cups water

3 tbsp extra virgin olive oil

lemon juice, to taste

Directions:

Heat olive oil in a deep soup pot and sauté leeks for 3-4 minutes. Add in potatoes and cook for a minute more.

Stir in water, bring to a boil, and add the brown rice. Reduce heat and simmer for 30 minutes.

Add lemon juice, to taste, and serve.

Mediterranean Chickpea Soup

Serves: 5-6
Prep time: 30 min

Ingredients:

1 can (15 oz) chickpeas, drained

1 small onion, chopped

2 garlic cloves, minced

1 can (15 oz) tomatoes, diced

2 cups vegetable broth

1 cup milk

3 tbsp extra virgin olive oil

2 bay leaves

1/2 tsp dried oregano

Directions:

Heat olive oil in a deep soup pot and sauté onion and garlic for 1-2 minutes. Add in broth, chickpeas, tomatoes, bay leaves, and oregano.

Bring the soup to a boil then reduce heat and simmer for 20 minutes. Add in milk and cook for 1-2 minutes more. Set aside to cool, discard the bay leaves and blend until smooth.

Carrot, Sweet Potato and Chickpea Soup

Serves: 4-5
Prep time: 25 min

Ingredients:

4 large carrots, chopped

1 small onion, chopped

1 can (15 oz) chickpeas, undrained

2 sweet potatoes, peeled and diced

4 cups vegetable broth

2 tbsp extra virgin olive oil

1 tsp cumin

1 tsp ginger

Directions:

Heat olive oil in a large saucepan over medium heat. Add onion and carrots and sauté until tender. Add in broth, chickpeas, sweet potato and seasonings.

Bring to a boil then reduce heat and simmer, covered, for 30 minutes. Blend soup until smooth, add coconut milk and cook for 2-3 minutes until heated through.

Mediterranean Lentil and Chickpea Soup

Serves: 4-5
Prep time: 20 min

Ingredients:

1 cup red lentils

2 carrots, chopped

1 onion, chopped

1 garlic clove, chopped

1 small red pepper, chopped

1 can tomatoes, chopped

½ can chickpeas, drained

½ can white beans, drained

1 celery stalk, chopped

6 cups water

1 tbsp paprika

1 tsp ginger, grated

1 tsp ground cumin

3 tbsp extra virgin olive oil

Directions:

Heat olive oil in a deep soup pot and gently sauté onions, garlic, red pepper and ginger. Add in water, lentils, chickpeas, white beans, tomatoes, carrots, celery, and cumin.

Bring to a boil then lower heat and simmer for 20 minutes, or until the lentils are tender. Purée half the soup in a food processor. Return the puréed soup to the pot, stir and serve.

Creamy Tomato and Roasted Pepper Soup

Serves: 4-5
Prep time: 35 min

Ingredients:

1 (12-ounce) jar roasted red peppers, drained and chopped

1 large onion, chopped

2 garlic cloves, minced

4 medium tomatoes, chopped

4 cups vegetable broth

3 tbsp extra virgin olive oil

2 bay leaves

Directions:

Heat olive oil in a large saucepan over medium-high heat and sauté onion for 3-4 minutes, stirring. Add in garlic and saute until just fragrant. Stir in the red peppers, bay leaves and tomatoes and simmer for 10 minutes.

Add broth, season with salt and pepper and bring to the boil. Reduce heat and simmer for 20 minutes.

Set aside to cool slightly, remove the bay leaves and blend, in batches, until smooth.

Fresh Asparagus Soup

Serves: 4-5
Prep time: 35 min

Ingredients:

2 lb fresh asparagus, cut into 1 inch pieces

1 large onion, chopped

2 garlic cloves, minced

½ cup raw cashews, soaked in warm water for 1 hour

3 cups vegetable broth

3 tbsp extra virgin olive oil

lemon juice, to taste

Directions:

Heat olive oil in a large saucepan over medium-high heat and sauté onion for 3-4 minutes, stirring. Add in garlic and saute until just fragrant.

Stir in asparagus and simmer for 5 minutes. Add broth, season with salt and pepper and bring to the boil. Reduce heat and simmer for 20 minutes.

Set aside to cool slightly, add cashews, and blend, in batches, until smooth. Season with lemon juice and serve.

Fast Red Lentil Soup

Serves: 4-5
Prep time: 15 min

Ingredients:

1 cup red lentils

1/2 small onion, chopped

2 garlic cloves, chopped

1/2 red pepper, chopped

3 cups vegetable broth

1 cup coconut milk

3 tbsp extra virgin olive oil

1 tbsp paprika

1/2 tsp ginger

1 tsp cumin

salt and black pepper, to taste

Directions:

Gently heat olive oil in a large saucepan. Add onion, garlic, red pepper, paprika, ginger and cumin and sauté, stirring, until just fragrant.

Add in red lentils and vegetable broth. Bring to a boil, cover, and simmer for 15 minutes. Add in coconut milk and simmer for 5 more minutes.

Remove from heat, season with salt and black pepper, and blend until smooth. Serve hot.

Curried Lentil and Parsnip Soup

Serves: 4-5
Prep time: 35 min

Ingredients:

1 cup red lentils

5 medium parsnips, peeled and cut into chunks

1 onion, chopped

1 garlic clove, chopped

2 large apples, peeled, cored and cut into chunks

6 cups vegetable broth

3 tbsp curry paste

3 tbsp extra virgin olive oil

Directions:

1 cup Greek yogurt, to serve

Heat olive oil in a deep soup pot and gently sauté onions, garlic and curry paste. Add the parsnips, lentils and apple pieces.

Pour over the vegetable broth and bring to a simmer. Cook for 30 minutes, or until the parsnips are soft and the lentils mushy.

Remove from the heat and purée the soup in a food processor. Return the to the pot, and serve with yogurt.

Indian Chickpea Soup

Serves: 4-5
Prep time: 20 min

Ingredients:

2 carrots, chopped

1 small onion, chopped

1 cup green beans, chopped

1 garlic clove, minced

1 can chickpeas, undrained

4 cups vegetable broth

3-4 tbsp extra virgin olive oil

1 tbsp garam masala

1 tsp finely grated fresh root ginger

salt and black pepper, to taste

naan bread, to serve

Directions:

Heat olive oil in a deep soup pot over medium-high heat. Gently sauté onion, garlic and carrots for 3-4 minutes, stirring. Add in ginger and gram masala and cook for 1 minute more, stirring.

Add vegetable broth and chickpeas. Bring to the boil then reduce heat and simmer, covered, for 15 minutes.

Blend soup until smooth and return to pan. Add in green beans and cook over medium-high heat for 3-5 minutes.

Season with salt and pepper to taste, and serve with naan bread.

Celery, Apple and Carrot Soup

Serves: 4-5
Prep time: 20 min

Ingredients:

2 celery stalks, chopped

1 large apple, chopped

1/2 onion, chopped

2 carrots, chopped

1 garlic clove, minced

4 cups vegetable broth

3-4 tbsp extra virgin olive oil

1 tsp paprika

1 tsp grated ginger

salt and black pepper, to taste

Directions:

Heat olive oil in a deep soup pot over medium-high heat. Gently sauté onion, garlic and carrots for 3-4 minutes, stirring. Add in paprika, ginger, celery, apple and broth.

Bring to the boil then reduce heat and simmer, covered, for 10 minutes. Blend soup until smooth and return to pan.

Cook over medium-high heat until heated through. Season with salt and pepper to taste and serve.

Pea, Dill and Rice Soup

Serves: 4
Prep time: 10 min

Ingredients:

1 (16 oz) bag frozen green peas

1 onion, chopped

3-4 garlic cloves, chopped

1/3 cup rice

3 tbsp fresh dill, chopped

3 tbsp extra virgin olive oil

fresh dill, finely chopped, to serve

salt and pepper, to taste

Directions:

Heat oil in a large saucepan over medium-high heat and sauté onion and garlic for 3-4 minutes.

Add in peas and vegetable broth and bring to the boil. Stir in rice, cover, reduce heat, and simmer for 15 minutes. Add dill, season with salt and pepper and serve sprinkled with fresh dill.

Minted Pea and Nettle Soup

Serves: 4
Prep time: 10 min

Ingredients:

1 onion, chopped

3-4 garlic cloves, chopped

4 cups vegetable broth

2 tbsp dried mint leaves

1 16 oz bag frozen green peas

about 20 nettle tops

3 tbsp extra virgin olive oil

fresh dill, finely chopped, to serve

Directions:

Heat oil in a large saucepan over medium-high heat and sauté onion and garlic for 3-4 minutes.

Add in dried mint, peas, washed nettles, and vegetable broth and bring to the boil. Cover, reduce heat, and simmer for 10 minutes.

Remove from heat and set aside to cool slightly, then blend in batches, until smooth. Return soup to saucepan over medium-low heat and cook until heated through.

Season with salt and pepper. Serve sprinkled with fresh dill.

Bean and Pasta Soup

Serves: 4-5
Prep time: 10-15 min

Ingredients:

1 onion, chopped

2 large carrots, chopped

2 garlic cloves, minced

1 cup cooked orzo

1 15 oz can white beans, rinsed and drained

1 15 oz can tomatoes, diced and undrained

1 cup baby spinach leaves

3 cups vegetable broth

1 tbsp paprika

1 tbsp dried mint

3 tbsp extra virgin olive oil

salt and black pepper, to taste

Directions:

Heat the olive oil over medium heat and gently sauté the onion, garlic and carrots. Add in tomatoes, broth, salt and pepper, and bring to a boil.

Reduce heat and cook for 5-10 minutes, or until the carrots are tender. Stir in orzo, beans and spinach, and simmer until spinach is wilted.

Tuscan Bean Soup

Serves: 4-5
Prep time: 10-15 min

Ingredients:

1 onion, chopped

1 large carrot, chopped

2 garlic cloves, minced

1 15 oz can white beans, rinsed and drained

1 cup spinach leaves, trimmed and washed

3 cups vegetable broth

1 tbsp paprika

1 tbsp dried mint

3 tbsp extra virgin olive oil

salt and black pepper, to taste

Directions:

Heat the olive oil over medium heat and gently sauté the onion, garlic and carrot. Add in beans, broth, salt and pepper and bring to a boil.

Reduce heat and cook for 10 minutes, or until the carrots are tender. Stir in spinach, and simmer for about 5 minutes, until spinach is wilted.

Lima Bean Soup

Serves: 5-6
Prep time: 3-4 hrs for soaking, 120 min for cooking

Ingredients:

1 lb dry Lima beans

4-5 cups water

2 leeks, white part only, chopped

1 small onion, finely cut

1 small celery stalk, chopped

3 carrots, chopped

5 cups vegetable broth

4 tbsp extra virgin olive oil

salt and black pepper, to taste

Directions:

Wash the Lima beans and soak them in water for a few hours. Discard the water, pour 3 cups of fresh water and cook the beans for an hour; discard this water too.

In a deep soup pot, heat olive oil and sauté the onion, leeks, celery and carrots until tender-crisp. Add 5 cups of vegetable broth and the Lima beans. Stir, bring to the boil, lower heat and simmer for 1 hour.

Season with salt and black pepper and purée half the soup in a food processor. Return the puréed soup to the pot, stir and serve.

Italian Vegetable Soup

Serves: 4-5
Prep time: 25 min

Ingredients:

1/2 onion, chopped

2 garlic cloves, chopped

¼ cabbage, chopped

1 carrot, chopped

2 celery stalks, chopped

3 cups water

1 cup canned tomatoes, diced, undrained

1 1/2 cup green beans, trimmed and cut into 1/2-inch pieces

1/2 cup pasta, cooked

2-3 fresh basil leaves

2 tbsp extra virgin olive oil

black pepper and salt, to taste

Directions:

Heat the olive oil in a large pot over medium-high heat. Add the onion and cook until translucent, about 4 minutes. Add in the garlic, carrot and celery and cook for 5 minutes more.

Stir in the green beans, cabbage, tomatoes, basil, and water and bring to a boil. Reduce heat and simmer uncovered, for 15 minutes, or until vegetables are tender.

Stir in pasta, season with pepper and salt to taste and serve.

French Vegetable Soup

Serves: 4-5
Prep time: 25 min

Ingredients:

2 leeks, white and pale green parts only, well rinsed and thinly sliced

1 large zucchini, peeled and diced

1 medium fennel bulb, trimmed, cored, and cut into large chunks

2 garlic cloves, chopped

3 cups vegetable broth

1 cup canned tomatoes, drained and chopped

1/2 cup vermicelli, broken into small pieces

3 tbsp extra virgin olive oil

black pepper, to taste

Directions:

Heat the olive oil in a large stockpot. Add the leeks and saute over low heat for 5 minutes. Add in the zucchini, fennel and garlic and cook for about 5 minutes.

Stir in the vegetable broth and the tomatoes and bring to the boil. Reduce heat and simmer, uncovered, for 20 minutes, or until the vegetables are tender but still holding their shape.

Stir in the vermicelli. Simmer for a further 5 minutes and serve.

Spiced Beet and Carrot Soup

Serves: 4-5
Prep time: 25 min

Ingredients:

3 beets, washed and peeled

2 carrots, peeled and chopped

1 small onion, chopped

1 garlic clove, chopped

3 cups vegetable broth

1 cup water

2 tbsp extra virgin olive oil

1 tsp grated ginger

1 tsp grated orange peel

Directions:

Heat the olive oil in a large stockpot. Add the onion and saute over low heat for 3-4 minutes or until translucent. Add the garlic, beets, carrots, ginger and lemon rind.

Stir in water and vegetable broth and bring to the boil. Reduce heat to medium and simmer, partially covered, for 30 minutes, or until beets are tender.

Cool slightly and blend soup in batches until smooth. Season with salt and pepper and serve.

Creamy Cauliflower Soup

Serves: 4-5
Prep time: 35 min

Ingredients:

1 medium head cauliflower, chopped

1 garlic clove, minced

3 cups vegetable broth

1 cup milk

3-4 tbsp extra virgin olive oil

salt, to taste

black pepper, to taste

Directions:

Heat the olive oil in a deep pot over medium heat and gently sauté the cauliflower for 4-5 minutes. Stir in the garlic and vegetable broth and bring to a boil. Reduce heat, cover, and simmer for 30 minutes.

Add in coconut milk and blend in a blender until smooth. Season with salt and pepper to taste and serve.

Pumpkin and Bell Pepper Soup

Serves: 4-5
Prep time: 35 min

Ingredients:

1/2 small onion, chopped

3 cups pumpkin cubes

2 red bell peppers, chopped

1 carrot, chopped

3 cups vegetable broth

3 tbsp extra virgin olive oil

1/2 tsp cumin

salt and black pepper, to taste

Directions:

Heat the olive oil in a deep soup pot and sauté the onion for 4-5 minutes. Add in the pumpkin, carrot and bell peppers and cook, stirring, for 5 minutes. Stir in broth and cumin and bring to the boil.

Reduce heat to low, cover, and simmer, stirring occasionally, for 30 minutes, or until vegetables are soft. Season with salt and pepper, blend in batches and reheat to serve.

Mushroom Soup

Serves: 4-5
Prep time: 35 min

Ingredients:

2 lbs mushrooms, peeled and chopped

1 large onion, chopped

2 garlic cloves, minced

3 cups vegetable broth

1 tsp dried thyme leaves

salt and pepper, to taste

3 tbsp extra virgin olive oil

Directions:

Sauté onions and garlic in a large soup pot until transparent. Add thyme and mushrooms.

Stir and cook for 10 minutes, then add the broth and simmer for another 10-20 minutes.

Blend, season with salt and black pepper, and serve.

Brown Lentil Soup

Serves: 4-5
Prep time: 35 min

Ingredients:

1 cup brown lentils

1 small onion, chopped

4 garlic cloves, minced

1 medium carrot, chopped

1 medium tomato, diced

3 cups warm water

4 tbsp extra virgin olive oil

1 tbsp paprika

1 tbsp summer savory

Directions:

Heat olive oil in a deep soup pot and cook the onions and carrots until tender. Add in paprika, garlic, lentils, savory and water, stir, and bring to the boil.

Reduce heat and cook, covered, for 30 minutes. Add the tomato and salt and simmer for 10 minutes more.

Slow Cooked Lentil, Barley and Mushroom Soup

Serves 4-5
Prep time: 4-8 hours

Ingredients:

2 medium leeks, trimmed, halved, sliced

10 white button mushrooms, sliced

3 garlic cloves, cut

2 bay leaves

2 cans tomatoes, chopped, undrained

3/4 cup red lentils

1/3 cup barley

5 cups water

1 tsp paprika

1 tsp savory

½ tsp cumin

Directions:

Combine all ingredients into slow cooker and season with salt and pepper to taste.

Cover and cook on high for 4 hours or on low for 8 hours.

Red Lentil and Quinoa Soup

Serves: 4
Prep time: 20 min

Ingredients:

½ cup quinoa

1 cup red lentils

5 cups water

1 onion, chopped

2-3 garlic cloves, chopped

½ red bell pepper, finely cut

1 small tomato, chopped

3 tbsp extra virgin olive oil

1 tsp ginger

1 tsp cumin

1 tbsp paprika

salt and black pepper, to taste

Directions:

Wash and drain quinoa and red lentils and set aside.

In a large soup pot, heat the olive oil over medium heat. Add the onion, garlic and red pepper and sauté for 1-2 minutes, stirring. Add the paprika and spices and stir.

Add in the red lentils and quinoa, stir and add the water. Gently bring to the boil, then lower heat and simmer, covered for 15 minutes. Add the tomato and cook for five more minutes. Blend the soup, serve and enjoy!

Spinach and Quinoa Soup

Serves: 4-5
Prep time: 20 min

Ingredients:

½ cup quinoa

1 onion, chopped

1 garlic clove, chopped

1 small zucchini, peeled and diced

1 tomato, diced

2 cups fresh spinach, cut

4 cups water

3 tbsp extra virgin olive oil

1 tbsp paprika

salt and pepper, to taste

Directions:

Heat olive oil in a deep soup pot over medium-high heat. Add onion and garlic and sauté for 1 minute, stirring constantly. Add in paprika and zucchini, stir, and cook for 2-3 minutes more.

Add 4 cups of water and bring to a boil then add in spinach and quinoa. Stir and reduce heat. Simmer for 15 minutes then set aside to cool.

Vegetable Quinoa Soup

Serves: 4-5
Prep time: 20 min

Ingredients:

½ cup quinoa

1 cup sliced leeks

1 garlic clove, chopped

½ carrot, diced

1 tomato, diced

1 small zucchini, diced

½ cup frozen green beans

4 cups water

1 tsp paprika

4 tbsp extra virgin olive oil

5-6 tbsp lemon juice, to serve

Directions:

Wash quinoa in a fine sieve under running water until the water runs clear. Set aside to drain.

Heat olive oil in a soup pot and gently sauté the leeks, garlic and carrot for 1 minute, stirring. Add paprika, zucchini, tomatoes, green beans and water.

Bring to a boil, add quinoa and lower heat to medium-low. Simmer for 15 minutes, or until the vegetables are tender. Serve with lemon juice.

Cabbage, Tomato and Pasta Soup

Serves: 4-5
Prep time: 30 min

Ingredients:

1 small onion, chopped

2 garlic cloves, chopped

1/2 head cabbage, shredded

1 carrot, chopped

3 large ripe tomatoes, diced

1/2 cup dried small pasta

4 cups chicken broth

1 tsp dried basil

1 tsp sugar

1 tbsp paprika

4 tbsp extra virgin olive oil

salt and pepper, to taste

Directions:

In a deep saucepan, heat the oil over medium heat and gently sauté the onion and garlic until fragrant. Add in the cabbage, carrot, tomatoes, paprika, basil and sugar and stir to coat well.

Add in the chicken broth and bring the soup to a boil, reduce heat, and simmer for 10 minutes. Stir in the pasta and cook for 15 minutes more. Season with salt and black pepper to taste and serve.

Slow Cooked Superfood Soup

Serves 4
Prep time: 5 min

Cooking time: 7 hours

Ingredients:

1 onion, chopped

2 garlic cloves, minced

2 carrots, chopped

1 turnip, diced

1 tomato, diced

1/4 cup dried lentils

2 cups chopped spinach

4 cups water

1/2 tsp dried basil

salt, to taste

black pepper, to taste

Directions:

Put all ingredients in the slow cooker. Cover and cook on high for 7 hours.

Turnip and Potato Soup

Serves 4-5
Prep time: 30 min

Ingredients:

1 onion, chopped

2 garlic cloves, minced

2 cups, diced potatoes

2 cups diced turnip

1 cup chopped kale

4 cups vegetable broth

1 cup heavy cream

3 tbsp extra virgin olive oil

1/2 tsp dried thyme

salt, to taste

black pepper, to taste

Directions:

Gently heat olive oil in a large saucepan over medium-high heat. Cook onion and garlic for 3-4 minutes until tender.

Add turnips, potatoes and the broth. Season with salt and black pepper to taste. Sprinkle with thyme and bring to a boil. Cover and simmer for 20 minutes or until the potato and turnip are tender.

Stir in the kale and the cream and allow to simmer together another 2-3 minutes.

FREE BONUS RECIPES: 20 Vegetarian Smoothies for Vibrant Health and Easy Weight Loss

Kale and Kiwi Smoothie

Serves: 2
Prep time: 2-3 min

Ingredients:

2-3 ice cubes

1 cup orange juice

1 small pear, peeled and chopped

2 kiwi, peeled and chopped

2-3 kale leaves

2-3 dates, pitted

Directions:

Combine all ingredients in a high speed blender and blend until smooth.

Delicious Broccoli Smoothie

Serves: 2
Prep time: 2-3 min

Ingredients:

2-3 frozen broccoli florets

1 cup coconut milk

1 banana, peeled and chopped

1 cup pineapple, cut

1 peach, chopped

1 tsp cinnamon

Directions:

Combine all ingredients in a high speed blender and blend until smooth.

Papaya Smoothie

Serves: 2
Prep time: 2-3 min

Ingredients:

2-3 frozen broccoli florets

1 cup orange juice

1 small ripe avocado, peeled, cored and diced

1 cup papaya

1 cup fresh strawberries

Directions:

Combine all ingredients in a high speed blender and blend until smooth.

Beet and Papaya Smoothie

Serves: 2
Prep time: 2-3 min

Ingredients:

3-4 ice cubes

1 cup orange juice

1 banana, peeled and chopped

1 cup papaya

1 small beet, peeled and cut

Directions:

Combine all ingredients in a high speed blender and blend until smooth.

Lean Green Smoothie

Serves: 2
Prep time: 2-3 min

Ingredients:

1 frozen banana, chopped

1 cup orange juice

2-3 kale leaves, stems removed

1 small cucumber, peeled and chopped

1/2 cup fresh parsley leaves

½ tsp grated ginger

Directions:

Combine all ingredients in a high speed blender and blend until smooth.

Easy Antioxidant Smoothie

Serves: 2
Prep time: 2-3 min

Ingredients:

2-3 frozen broccoli florets

1 cup orange juice

2 plums, cut

1 cup raspberries

1 tsp ginger powder

Directions:

Combine all ingredients in a high speed blender and blend until smooth.

Healthy Purple Smoothie

Serves: 2
Prep time: 2-3 min

Ingredients:

2-3 frozen broccoli florets

1 cup water

1/2 avocado, peeled and chopped

3 plums, chopped

1 cup blueberries

Directions:

Combine all ingredients in a high speed blender and blend until smooth.

Mom's Favorite Kale Smoothie

Serves: 2
Prep time: 2-3 min

Ingredients:

2-3 ice cubes

1½ cup orange juice

1 green small apple, cut

½ cucumber, chopped

2-3 leaves kale

½ cup raspberries

Directions:

Combine all ingredients in a high speed blender and blend until smooth.

Creamy Green Smoothie

Serves: 2
Prep time: 2-3 min

Ingredients:

1 frozen banana

1 cup coconut milk

1 small pear, chopped

1 cup baby spinach

1 cup grapes

1 tbsp coconut butter

1 tsp vanilla extract

Directions:

Combine all ingredients in a high speed blender and blend until smooth.

Strawberry and Arugula Smoothie

Serves: 2
Prep time: 2-3 min

Ingredients:

2 cups frozen strawberries

1 cup unsweetened almond milk

10-12 arugula leaves

1/2 tsp ground cinnamon

Directions:

Combine ice, almond milk, strawberries, arugula and cinnamon in a high speed blender. Blend until smooth and serve.

Emma's Amazing Smoothie

Serves: 2
Prep time: 2-3 min

Ingredients:

1 frozen banana, chopped

1 cup orange juice

1 large nectarine, sliced

1/2 zucchini, peeled and chopped

2-3 dates, pitted

Directions:

Combine all ingredients in a high speed blender and blend until smooth.

Good-To-Go Morning Smoothie

Serves: 2
Prep time: 2-3 min

Ingredients:

1 cup frozen strawberries

1 cup apple juice

1 banana, chopped

1 cup raw asparagus, chopped

1 tbsp ground flaxseed

Directions:

Combine all ingredients in a high speed blender and blend until smooth.

Endless Energy Smoothie

Serves: 2
Prep time: 2-3 min

Ingredients:

1 frozen banana, chopped

11/2 cup green tea

1 cup chopped pineapple

2 raw asparagus spears, chopped

1 lime, juiced

1 tbsp chia seeds

Directions:

Combine all ingredients in a high speed blender and blend until smooth.

High-fibre Fruit Smoothie

Serves: 2
Prep time: 2-3 min

Ingredients:

1 frozen banana, chopped

1 cup orange juice

2 cups chopped papaya

1 cup shredded cabbage

1 tbsp chia seeds

Directions:

Combine all ingredients in a high speed blender and blend until smooth.

Nutritious Green Smoothie

Serves: 2
Prep time: 2-3 min

Ingredients:

2-3 frozen broccoli florets

1 cup apple juice

1 large pear, chopped

1 kiwi, peeled and chopped

1 cup spinach leaves

1-2 dates, pitted

Directions:

Combine all ingredients in a high speed blender and blend until smooth.

Apricot, Strawberry and Banana Smoothie

Serves: 2
Prep time: 2-3 min

Ingredients:

1 frozen banana

11/2 cup almond milk

5 dried apricots

1 cup fresh strawberries

Directions:

Combine all ingredients in a high speed blender and blend until smooth.

Spinach and Green Apple Smoothie

Serves: 2
Prep time: 2-3 min

Ingredients:

3-4 ice cubes

1 cup unsweetened almond milk

1 banana, peeled and chopped

2 green apples, peeled and chopped

1 cup raw spinach leaves

3-4 dates, pitted

1 tsp grated ginger

Directions:

Combine all ingredients in a high speed blender and blend until smooth.

Superfood Blueberry Smoothie

Serves: 2
Prep time: 2-3 min

Ingredients:

2-3 cubes frozen spinach

1 cup green tea

1 banana

2 cups blueberries

1 tbsp ground flaxseed

Directions:

Combine all ingredients in a high speed blender and blend until smooth.

Zucchini and Blueberry Smoothie

Serves: 2
Prep time: 2-3 min

Ingredients:

1 cup frozen blueberries

1 cup unsweetened almond milk

1 banana

1 zucchini, peeled and chopped

Directions:

Combine all ingredients in a high speed blender and blend until smooth.

Tropical Spinach Smoothie

Serves: 2
Prep time: 2-3 min

Ingredients:

1/2 cup crushed ice or 3-4 ice cubes

1 cup coconut milk

1 mango, peeled and diced

1 cup fresh spinach leaves

4-5 dates, pitted

1/2 tsp vanilla extract

Directions:

Combine all ingredients in a high speed blender and blend until smooth.

About the Author

Alissa Grey is a fitness and nutrition enthusiast who loves to teach people about losing weight and feeling better about themselves. She lives in a small French village in the foothills of a beautiful mountain range with her husband, three teenage kids, two free spirited dogs, and various other animals.

Alissa is incredibly lucky to be able to cook and eat natural foods, mostly grown nearby, something she's done since she was a teenager. She enjoys yoga, running, reading, hanging out with her family, and growing organic vegetables and herbs.

Printed in Great Britain
by Amazon

44507116R00037